I'M AN ADVANCED WEB PAGE CODER

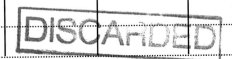

Max Wainewright

WAYLAND

CONTENTS

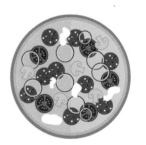

INTRODUCTION

In this book, you will learn how to code your own amazing web pages using HTML. HTML stands for Hyper Text Mark Up Language and is the language used to build web pages. You'll find out how to add text, images, links and even video to a web page. Once you have completed all the projects, you will be on your way to becoming an HTML expert!

There are lots of different tools you can use to build web pages:

You could use a simple text editor – a program that lets you enter, change and store text.

This will work fine but can be quite fiddly, as the software won't give you any help.

page.html

```
<html>
<p>My text</p>
```

There are many internet sites and blogging tools. These online tools will quickly build a web page, but you won't learn much about HTML.

The best thing to use for the activities in this book is an offline HTML editor, like Sublime Text. This will support you as you type your code, but also give you the opportunity to learn the actual HTML code.

There are two separate windows that you'll be using:

Sublime Text

```
<html>
  <h1>The Forest</h1>
  <img src='tree.jpg'>
</html>
```

The text editor to make your HTML page.

Web Browser

The Forest
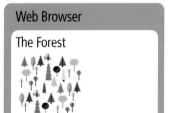

The browser to view your HTML page.

Read through each page of this book, and then try the activities. You'll learn how to put the basic elements on a web page and then add interest with different colours and font sizes. Towards the end of the book, you'll be able to do some amazing projects and even create your own mini-websites.

⟩ GETTING STARTED

There are lots of ways to create an HTML file. There will probably be a simple text editor already on your computer called Notepad (if you have Windows), or TextEdit (on a Mac). This will help you get started, but it will be easier to create HTML if you download a more powerful text editor. In this book, we will use a text editor called Sublime Text. There are many other text editors you could download, such as Brackets or Notepad++ – all of these are free for you to try out.

STEP 1 – FIND THE SUBLIME TEXT WEBSITE ▶

⇨ Open your web browser and visit **www.sublimetext.com**

www.sublimetext.com

STEP 2 – START DOWNLOADING ▶

⇨ Click the **Download** button near the top of the web page.

Download

⇨ Choose which version you need. If you are not sure, then ask an adult to help you. Click the Apple menu, then **About** if you are using a Mac. On a PC, click the **Start** menu, select **System**, and click **About**.

⇨ Wait for the download to complete.

STEP 3 – INSTALL THE SOFTWARE ▶

⇨ Some web browsers will then ask you to run the installation program. Choose **Run**.

⇨ If this does not happen, don't panic. The installer file should have been downloaded to your computer.

Look in your **Downloads** folder for it. Double-click it to start installing your new text editor. You should get a big grey box giving you instructions on what to do next. Follow these instructions to complete the installation.

WHY DO WE NEED HTML?

There are over 600 million active web pages in the world. HTML is the universal language that is used to create all of these web pages.

A special program called a browser is used to view a web page. Commonly used browsers include Chrome, Internet Explorer, Safari and Firefox.

HTML pages can contain different things, including text, graphics, tables, headings, buttons, links and videos. Each of these separate things is called an element.

Each element has tags and content. The tag explains what type of element to display and the content tells the browser what to display inside that element.

STEP 4 – RUNNING SUBLIME TEXT

On a PC:

⇨ Click **Start** > **Programs** > **Sublime Text**. Or just click **Sublime Text** if it appears in the 'recently added' section.

On a Mac:

⇨ Click **Finder**.

⇨ Click **Applications**.

Applications

⇨ Make a shortcut by dragging **Sublime Text** from **Finder** on to your dock at the bottom of the **Desktop**.

⇨ Click the **Sublime Text** icon.

STEP 5 – YOUR FIRST PAGE

⇨ Carefully type this into your text editor for lines 1, 2 and 3:

Sublime Text

```
<html>
<p>Welcome</p>
</html>
```

Start all HTML files with <html>.

Show a paragraph saying 'Welcome'.

End all HTML files with </html>.

STEP 6 – SAVE YOUR PAGE

⇨ Click **File** > **Save**.

⇨ Save to your **Documents** folder.

⇨ Type **welcome.html** as the filename.

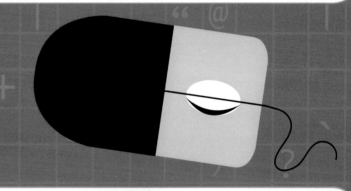

STEP 7 – VIEW YOUR PAGE

⇨ Open your **Documents** folder.

⇨ Find the **welcome.html** file and double-click it.

 Your very first web page should now load in your normal web browser! It should look something like this:

Documents/welcome.html

Welcome

TAGS

• Tags always start with < and end with >. These are known as angle brackets.

• All elements have an opening tag. and most have a closing tag.

KEY CONCEPT

Opening tag   Closing tag

<p>Welcome</p>

Content

❯HEADINGS AND PARAGRAPHS

Now you know how to make a very simple HTML web page, let's experiment and add some other elements to the page. We'll start by looking at how to add special text elements called headings.

STEP 1 – START YOUR TEXT EDITOR

On a PC:

⇨ Click **Start > Programs > Sublime Text.**

On a Mac:

⇨ Click the **Sublime Text** icon.

STEP 2 – ENTER THIS HTML

⇨ Carefully type this into your text editor for lines 1 to 6:

Sublime Text

<html>	Start the web page.
<h1>My Timetable</h1>	Add main heading.
<p>Maths</p>	Add first paragraph.
<p>English</p>	Add second paragraph.
<p>Science</p>	Add third paragraph.
</html>	End the web page.

STEP 3 – SAVE YOUR PAGE

⇨ Click **File** > **Save**.

⇨ Save to your **Documents** folder.

⇨ Type **timetable.html** as the filename.

STEP 4 – VIEW YOUR PAGE

⇨ Open your **Documents** folder.

⇨ Find the **timetable.html** file and double-click it.

⇨ Your web page should now load in your browser.

⇨ Notice how the **<h1>** heading tag has made the heading text large and bold.

Documents/timetable.html

My Timetable
Maths
English
Science

STEP 5 – ARRANGE YOUR SCREEN

As you start to develop more complex HTML pages, you need to be able to see the code and the HTML page at the same time.

⇨ Resize your text editor and browser windows so your screen looks like this whenever you are working on projects in HTML:

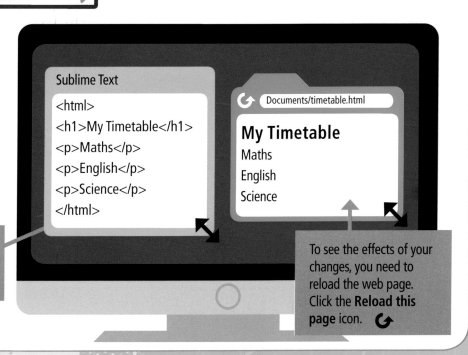

Sublime Text

```
<html>
<h1>My Timetable</h1>
<p>Maths</p>
<p>English</p>
<p>Science</p>
</html>
```

Documents/timetable.html

My Timetable
Maths
English
Science

If you make a change to your HTML in the text editor, save your file.

To see the effects of your changes, you need to reload the web page. Click the **Reload this page** icon. ↻

CUSTOMISE

• Change the timetable so it matches your own.

• Add to the timetable so it includes every day of the week.

• Experiment with other heading tags, from **<h1>** down to **<h6>**.

• Remember to use closing tags too **</h6>**.

STEP 6 – SUB-HEADINGS

⇨ Change your code so it has sub-headings for Monday and Tuesday:

Sublime Text

```
<html>
<h1>My Timetable</h1>
<h3>Monday</h3>
<p>Maths</p>
<p>English</p>
<h3>Tuesday</h3>
<p>Science</p>
<p>History</p>
</html>
```

Insert an <h3> sub-heading that says Monday. Don't forget the closing tag </h3>. When you add the / in the closing tag, most editors will finish the tag for you.

Add another <h3> element for Tuesday. Close it with the tag </h3>

Add more paragraphs to show other subjects.

  Now view your new web page!

KEY CONCEPT

HEADINGS

• Use **<h1>** and **</h1>** tags to show important headings on your pages. Use other tags, such as **<h3>**, for less significant headings.

⟩ A TOUCH OF COLOUR

Colour can be very useful as a way of drawing people's attention to different things and to explain what different buttons may do. In this activity, we will learn how to change the colour of HTML elements.

STEP 1 – START A NEW HTML FILE ▷

⇨ Start your text editor, or click **File** > **New File**.

STEP 2 – ADD YOUR CODE ▷

⇨ Carefully type this into your text editor:

Sublime Text

```
<html>                              Start the web page.
<h1>Invitation List</h1>            Add main heading.
<p style="color:red;">Alex</p>      Type very carefully,
<p style="color:green;">Anna</p>      adding all quotes,
<p style="color:blue;">Max</p>       colons and semi-colons.
</html>                             End the web page.
```

STEP 3 – SAVE YOUR PAGE ▷

⇨ Click **File** > **Save**.

⇨ Browse to your **Documents** folder.

⇨ Type **colours.html** as the filename.

STEP 4 – VIEW YOUR PAGE ▷

⇨ Open your **Documents** folder and double-click the **colours.html** file.

Documents/colours.html

Invitation List
_____
_____
_____

 Now view your new web page!

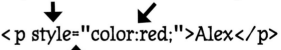 KEY CONCEPT

STYLE ATTRIBUTES

To tell the browser what colour our text will be, we add extra information to the paragraph tags. This is done by adding a style attribute to the opening tag of the HTML element.

Remember the equals sign, double quotes, colons and semi-colon as well as the angle brackets for the tags! Don't forget to use the US spelling of colour: color.

Style attribute   The value we want to give it
        ↓   ↘
< p style="color:red;">Alex</ p>
              ↑
        The property we are setting

CUSTOMISE

⇨ Now add more paragraphs with different names and different colours. Try out light or dark colours, for example **darkblue** or **lightgreen**.

⇨ Remember to click **File** > **Save** in the text editor, then refresh your browser.

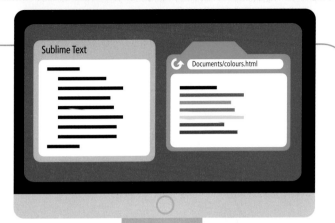

16 MILLION COLOURS

There is another, more precise, way to set colours, using a method that mixes together red, green and blue light. A number is given between 0 and 255 for the amount of red, green and blue in each colour, giving over 16 million combinations. This is called the RGB colour system.

The code to show bright red is 255,0,0. The red value is 255, green is 0 and blue is 0. The RGB value is then converted into a special code called hexadecimal, which uses the letters A to F instead of 10 to 15. The hexadecimal code for red is: #FF0000.

Don't worry if you don't understand all that yet, just try using these colour codes and experiment!

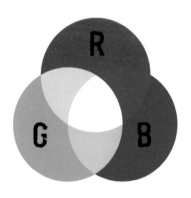

Hexadecimal codes must start with a hashtag # symbol. The letters of the code can be capital or lower case.

Colour	Red	Green	Blue	Hex code
Red	255	0	0	FF0000
Green	0	255	0	00FF00
Blue	0	0	255	0000FF
Purple	128	0	128	800080
White	255	255	255	FFFFFF
Black	0	0	0	000000
Yellow	255	255	0	FFFF00

⇨ Edit your text, changing the names, and using hexadecimal values instead of colour names.

Sublime Text

```
<html>
<h1>Invitation List</h1>
<p style="color:#FF8C00;">Jo</p>
<p style="color:#800080;">Maria</p>
<p style="color:#FFFF00;">Paul</p>
</html>
```

PHOTOGRAPHS AND PICTURES

We've seen how colour can be used to make web pages more interesting and informative. Pictures and photos are another really important element used in web pages. To add photos to a web page we need to use the image tag, **<img>**. We're going to create an animal web page, like the one below.

STEP 1 – PLANNING

⇨ Decide what images you would like to display on your web page. They can be photographs or other pictures.

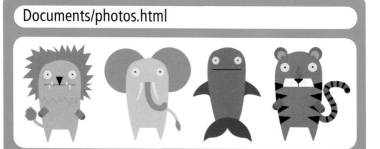

Documents/photos.html

STEP 2 – FIND A PICTURE

⇨ Find the images you have decided to use. They need to be placed in the same folder as your HTML file. If you are using a photo of your own, copy it and paste it into the **Documents** folder. Alternatively, find one by searching online, then save and download it. (See page 23 for information about using other people's photos in your projects.)

STEP 3 – CHECK!

⇨ Open your **Documents** folder and check the picture file is there. Depending on your browser and the photo, it may be called **lion.jpg**, **download.jpeg** or **download.jpg**.

⇨ If it is not there, go back to step 2 and try again.

STEP 4 – START A NEW HTML FILE

⇨ Carefully type this into your text editor:

Sublime Text

```
<html>                          Start the web page.
<img src='lion.jpeg'>           Use image filename as the URL.
</html>                         End the web page.
```

STEP 5 – SAVE YOUR PAGE ▶

⇨ Click **File** > **Save**.

⇨ Save to your **Documents** folder.

⇨ Type **photos.html** as the filename. The **photos.html** file must be in the same folder as your photo.

STEP 6 – VIEW YOUR PAGE ▶

⇨ Go to your **Documents** folder and double-click the **photos.html** file.

Documents/photos.html

If you type the code incorrectly or get the filename wrong, you may see this icon instead of the photo. Check your code carefully. Save it again and refresh.

STEP 7 – MORE IMAGES ▶

⇨ Repeat step 2 to add more photos to your **Documents** folder. Repeat steps 3 to 5, adding the code to show your new images.

Sublime Text

```html
<html>
<img src='lion.jpeg'>
<img src='elephant.jpeg'>
<img src='dolphin.jpeg'>
<img src='tiger.jpeg'>
</html>
```

Start the web page.

⎱ Add the img tags for your new photos one at a time.

End the web page.

 Save and **Reload** to see your page of photos.

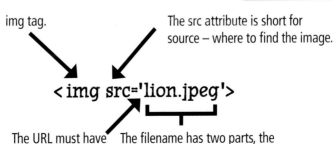

◤ **KEY CONCEPT**

IMAGES

To add photos and pictures to a web page, we need to use the image tag, `<img>`. The image tag is unusual, as it has no closing tag.

img tag.

The src attribute is short for source – where to find the image.

< img src='lion.jpeg'>

The URL must have quotes around it.

The filename has two parts, the name (lion) and its type (jpeg).

> STYLE AND CSS

You now know how to add the basic elements of text and images to a web page. Let's have another look at how to change the appearance of multiple elements on the page, using a couple of lines of code. This gives a smart look to your page and makes your code more reliable and adaptable.

STEP 1 – PLANNING

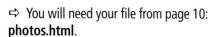

Documents/stylish.html

⇨ Decide how you would like to present your images.

⇨ Think about adding borders and using different colours in the style section.

STEP 2 – OPEN PHOTOS.HTML

⇨ You will need your file from page 10: **photos.html**.

⇨ Open your text editor and browse to find the file.

⇨ Click **File** > **Save As** and rename the file as **stylish.html**

STEP 3 – CHECK IT

⇨ Open your **Documents** folder. Find the new **stylish.html** file and double-click on it. Check your new file appears in the browser.

⇨ Arrange your screen in the usual way with the text editor on the left and browser on the right.

STYLE SHEETS

The code language we use to say what goes on a web page is called HTML. The language we use to describe how these elements will look onscreen is called CSS. CSS stands for **Cascading Style Sheets**.

There are three main ways we can use CSS:

- **Inline styling** where we put the styling information inside the opening tag of paragraph elements (see page 8)

- **Internal Style Sheets** where we put the styling information within the web page (see page 13)

- **External Style Sheets** allows you to change the appearance of the whole site just by changing one file. This is a separate file that each page has a link to.

⇨ Put the cursor after **<html>** and press enter a few times to make some space. Insert the code highlighted below. This will give all the images a solid black border, 8 pixels thick. They will also have a margin of 8 pixels around them and they will be 90 pixels high.

Sublime Text

```
<html>
<style>
    img{border:8px solid black;
    margin:8px; height:90px;}
    body{background-color:orange;}
</style>
<img src='lion.jpeg'>
<img src='elephant.jpeg'>
<img src='dolphin.jpeg'>
<img src='tiger.jpeg'>
</html>
```

Start the style section.

> Add an image border of 8 pixels, a margin of 8 pixels and make the images 90 pixels high.

> Add an orange background colour to the page.

End the style section.

⇨ You must type the code very carefully, using the curly brackets {}, semi-colons and colons. It doesn't matter if you press enter or not after each of the semi-colons.

STEP 5 – TEST IT

⇨ Click **File** > **Save** in the text editor, then **Reload** your browser.

 View your web page. Does it look similar to the illustration at the beginning of page 12?

CUSTOMISE

• Try changing the colours used in the style section.

• Vary the size of the margin and the image height.

• Use dotted instead of solid lines for the border.

• Add some paragraphs to label the photos. Set the colour of these by adding p{color:blue;} to the style section.

 A pixel is a picture element – one of millions of tiny grid squares used to create a picture on screen.

▲ **KEY CONCEPT**

STYLE

Use a <style> section to include some CSS. This will set the look of multiple elements on the page, without you having to repeat the code again.

⟩ LINKING IT TOGETHER

We get to another page of a book by simply turning the page. However, most web pages are linked to other pages by hyperlinks, or links for short. On the web, we either type in a new address or click on one of these links.

STEP 1 – START A NEW HTML FILE ▶

⇨ Carefully type this into your text editor:

```
Sublime Text
<html>
<h1>My Links</h1>
<a href='http://www.bbc.co.uk'>BBC</a>
<br>
<a href='http://www.youtube.com'>Youtube</a>
<br>
</html>
```

Add a simple heading.

Start the anchor tag <a. Then add href to set the URL and link to the BBC.

Link to Youtube.

Add a line break <br>. It starts a new line in the browser, leaving a gap between links.

⇨ Save your page in the **Documents** folder.

⇨ Type **links.html** as the filename.

STEP 2 – TEST YOUR PAGE ▶

⇨ Go to your **Documents** folder and double-click the **links.html** file.

⇨ Click to test each link. It should jump to the website shown. ➡

Documents/links.html

My Links

BBC
YouTube

⇨ Click the back button to return to your page.

⟨14⟩

⇨ Web pages don't use just text as links – many also use an icon or image. To use an image as a link:

Sublime Text

```html
<html>
<h1>My Links</h1>
<a href='http://www.bbc.co.uk'>BBC</a>
<br>
<a href='http://www.youtube.com'>Youtube</a>
<br>
<a href='https://www.zsl.org/'>
<img src='lion.jpeg'>
</a>
</html>
```

⇨ Click before the last line **</html>** and press enter a few times to make some space.

⇨ Add all the code highlighted in green.

⇨ Instead of using text as the link, use one of the photos you downloaded on page 10.

⇨ **Save** the page and **Reload** your browser.

CUSTOMISE

• Create groups of links, for example links to information about one of your hobbies. Use sub-headings to label them.

• Add a style section to the web page and change the appearance of the images you use and the background.

My Links

BBC
YouTube

My Links

BBC
YouTube

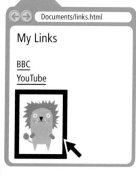

When you click on the picture of a lion, it should take you to London Zoo's website.

KEY CONCEPT

USING HYPERLINKS

The link starts with an opening anchor tag <a>.

The link ends with a closing anchor tag </a>.

```
<a href='http://www.bbc.co.uk'>BBC</a>
```

The **href** attribute is used to set the URL the link will jump to.

The **URL** (address) is typed here between the quotes.

The text for the link to display.

⟩ INPUT ELEMENTS

In addition to showing information, many web pages ask the user to enter various details. In this activity, we will look at different forms of input elements that ask for information. Our site won't be online and it won't save anything, so don't worry about what you type in.

STEP 1 – PLANNING

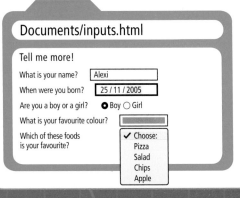

Documents/inputs.html

Tell me more!

What is your name?   Alexi
When were you born?   25 / 11 / 2005
Are you a boy or a girl?   ● Boy ○ Girl
What is your favourite colour?
Which of these foods
is your favourite?   ✔ Choose:
                              Pizza
                              Salad
                              Chips
                              Apple

⇨ Decide which questions you want to ask visitors to your web page.

STEP 2 – START A NEW HTML FILE

⇨ Carefully type this into your text editor:

```
Sublime Text

<html>
<h2>Tell me more!</h2>
<label>What is your name?</label>
<input type="text">
</html>
```
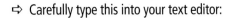

Add the basic text input box. It has no closing tag.

Add a heading.

Add a label. This is similar to the paragraph element, but the next element will still be on the same line.

⇨ Save your page in the **Documents** folder.

⇨ Type **inputs.html** as the filename.

STEP 3 – TEST YOUR PAGE

⇨ Double-click the **inputs.html** file in your **Documents** folder.

The user adds their name here.

Documents/welcome.html

Tell me more!

What is your name?

CUSTOMISE

• Think of some more questions to add. Which type of input would be best for each one?

• Add a style section.

⇨ Here is the code for the whole page. Click before **</html>** and press enter to make some space. Try adding the code one input element at a time, then **Save** and test each time.

```
Sublime Text

<html>
    <h2>Tell me more!</h2>

    <label>What is your name?</label>
    <input type="text">
    <br><br>

    <label>When were you born?</label>
    <input type="date">
    <br><br>

    <label>Are you a boy or a girl?</label>
    <input type="radio" name="bg">Boy
    <input type="radio" name="bg">Girl
    <br><br>

    <label>What is your favourite colour?</label>
    <input type="color">
    <br><br>

    <label>Which of these foods is your favourite?</label>
    <select>
        <option>Choose:</option>
        <option>Pizza</option>
        <option>Salad</option>
        <option>Chips</option>
        <option>Apple</option>
    </select>
</html>
```

Add a blank line with a <br> element. This gap just makes our code clearer!

Set up a date picker, which contains a list of dates to choose from.

Add a radio button. It is a good type of input to use if there are only a limited number of choices. The code name="bg" links the two options together.

Set up a colour picker, which contains different colours to choose from. Each browser will present this differently.

Create a drop-down menu.

Add options for the drop-down menu.

Add a closing tag for the drop-down.

 Save and **Reload** to see your web page. Ask a friend to answer the questions.

INDENTING
Each paragraph in a book is usually indented. Text editors often automatically indent parts of your code to make it easier to read (see the last section of code above).

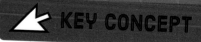 KEY CONCEPT

INPUT AND SELECT ELEMENTS
There are a variety of input elements that can be used to get information from the person viewing a web page. Another way is to use a select element by creating a drop-down menu.

› EMBEDDING VIDEO

You may want to add videos to your web pages. Linking to a video on another website is one way to do this, but you might prefer to keep people on your web page. The best way to do this is to embed the video.

Some videos (particularly music videos) will look as though they are embedded, but when you click them they will act as a link. This is just how the video owners have asked the video to be hosted.

STEP I – PLANNING

Documents/video.html

Watch Video

How a computer works

0:46 / 4:02

This is a hyperlink (see page 15) that links to the page with the video on.

This is the same video, but embedded on the web page within an **<iframe>**.

LINKING TO A VIDEO

STEP 2 – GET THE VIDEO URL

⇨ Choose a video from YouTube or a similar website.

www.youtube.com/watch=v

www.youtube.com/watch=v

⇨ Click the URL in the address bar at the top. Make sure it is all highlighted.

⇨ Right-click on the URL.

| Cut |
| **Copy** |
| Paste |

⇨ Click **Copy**.

STEP 3 – START A NEW HTML FILE

Sublime Text

```
<html>
<a href='https://www.youtube.com/watch?v=J8hzJxb0rpc'>
Watch Video
</a>
</html>
```

Click Edit > Paste to add the URL. (Don't try to type it in!)

Remember to close the link with </a> and </html> to show the end of the page.

⇨ Click **File > Save**.   ⇨ **Save** to **Documents**.   ⇨ Type **video.html** as the filename.

STEP 4 – TEST

⇨ Double-click the **video.html** file in your **Documents** folder.

Documents/video.html

Watch Video

⇨ Click the link and you should jump to the page with your chosen video.

CUSTOMISE

• Find another video and click **Share**. Before you copy the embed code, try experimenting with the options that set the size of the video.

• Add other elements, such as headings and titles, to the page.

• Add a style section to add colour to the page.

EMBEDDING A VIDEO

STEP I – GET THE EMBED CODE

⇨ Choose a video from YouTube or another similar website.

 Share

⇨ Click the **Share** button. (Look in the middle, below the video.)

Embed

⇨ Click the **Embed** button.

llowfullscreen></iframe>

⇨ Right-click the embed code.

⇨ Click **Copy**.

STEP 2 – START A NEW HTML

⇨ Add **<html>** and then press **enter**. **</html>** shows the end of the HTML.

⇨ Click **Edit > Paste** to add the embed code. You will see that the embed code includes **<iframe>** and **</iframe>**.

```
Sublime Text

<html>
<iframe width="560" height="315"
src="https://www.youtube.com/embed/J8hzJxb0rpc?rel=0
&amp;controls=0&amp;showinfo=0" frameborder="0"
allowfullscreen></iframe>
</html>
```

⇨ Click **File > Save**.

⇨ Save to **Documents**.

⇨ Type **video2.html** as the filename.

STEP 3 – TEST

⇨ Double-click the **video2.html** file in your **Documents** folder.

Documents/video2.html

Your video should now appear, embedded in your own web page. Try playing it!

KEY CONCEPT

IFRAMES

iframes can be used to include content, such as videos, from another site on your own web page.

FAVOURITE MOVIE CLIPS

In this project, you will use iframes and embedded video to create a page of your favourite movie clips or trailers. Use headings and paragraphs to label each clip and add a style section to make the page look really cool. You could even try adding a special background to the page.

STEP I – PLANNING

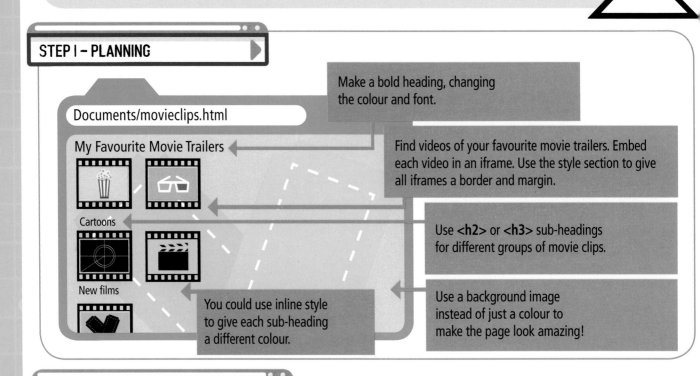

Documents/movieclips.html

My Favourite Movie Trailers

Cartoons

New films

Make a bold heading, changing the colour and font.

Find videos of your favourite movie trailers. Embed each video in an iframe. Use the style section to give all iframes a border and margin.

Use **<h2>** or **<h3>** sub-headings for different groups of movie clips.

You could use inline style to give each sub-heading a different colour.

Use a background image instead of just a colour to make the page look amazing!

STEP 2 – USING A BACKGROUND IMAGE

We have looked at how to set the background colour (see page 13) and how to download images to use in a web page. You can also combine these techniques to set a background image for the whole page.

⇨ Find a file you want to use – try an image search for 'background textures'.

⇨ Right-click and **Save** the file.

Type the name of your file here. Remember the quotes.

⇨ Make a style section in your HTML and add in this code:

```
body{background-image: url('my-bg.png');}
```

Type the letters url as well as the filename of the background image.

⇨ Make sure you include all the code: the curly brackets {}, colon, normal brackets and semi-colon.

⇨ Start your text editor and click **File** > **New File**.

⇨ Here is the code for the whole page. Rather than typing it all in at once, start with both HTML tags, then the headings. After that, copy an embed code for one video (see page 18) and try pasting it in. Save it as **movieclips.html**. Preview and test your file in your browser.

Sublime Text

```
<html>

<style>
    body{background-image: url('my-bg.png');}
    h1{font-family:Tahoma; margin:20px;}
    h2{font-family:Tahoma; margin:20px;}
    iframe{margin:20px; border:black solid 20px;}
</style>

<h1>My Favourite Movie Trailers</h1>
<iframe ...></iframe>
<iframe ...></iframe>

<h2 style='color:Green;'>Cartoons</h2>
<iframe ...></iframe>
<iframe ...></iframe>

<h2 style='color:Magenta;'>New films</h2>
<iframe ...></iframe>

</html>
```

Start the style section.
Set the page background.
Choose a font and margin size for your headings (20px means 20 pixels).

Add this style to iframe to give each video a black border around it.

Add the main heading.

Copy the embed code from the video website and paste it in place of the highlighted code.

Add inline styling for each h2 heading.

Paste in the embed codes in place of the highlighted code. (See page 19.)

Remember to close the web page with </html>.

Keep saving and reloading to test your code as you are typing it in.

CUSTOMISE

• Use all the techniques you have learnt so far to make the page look just as you want it!

• Change colours, fonts and sizes, or add other images.

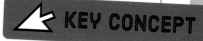
KEY CONCEPT

FONT FAMILY

You can choose the font a paragraph or heading element uses. CSS calls this setting the **font-family**.

p{font-family: Arial;}
p{font-family: 'Times New Roman';}

Use quotes if the font has any spaces in its name.

> IMAGE GALLERY

We have looked at how to make images into links (see page 15). We will extend this idea by creating an image gallery. Your image gallery could have any theme, but we will use famous landmarks as our focus here.

STEP I – PLANNING

Documents/landmarks.html

Famous Landmarks

Use CSS to style the heading.

Clicking one of the small images (called a thumbnail) will take you to the large version of the image.

Use a background image instead of just a colour to make the page stand out.

Style the images to give them a border (or frame) and margin between each one.

CUSTOMISE

• Experiment with different colours, fonts and sizes.

• Add sections to your page – try adding sub-headings for each continent the landmarks are found in.

STEP 2 – GET THE URL OF A PICTURE

You need to choose a photo to use. However, instead of downloading the picture, you need to copy the URL (address) of the picture on the web.

Eiffel Tower

Search

View Image

⇨ Go online and search for a photo of the Eiffel Tower.

⇨ Choose a photo and click it.

⇨ Click it again to get a larger version. If you see a **View Image** button, click it.

⇨ Right-click the photo.

⇨ Click **Copy Image Address**.

⇨ Start your text editor or click **File** > **New File**.

⇨ Here is the code for the whole page. Rather than typing it all in at once, start with both HTML tags, then the headings. After that, copy an embed code for one image and try pasting it in. Save it as **landmarks.html**. Preview and test your file in your browser. See page 14 for help with making links.

Sublime Text

```
<html>

<style>
    h1{font-family: Verdana;}
    body{background-image: url('bg1.png');}
    img{margin:10px; height:160px;
        border:white solid 20px;}
</style>

<h1>Famous Landmarks</h1>

<a href='PASTE PICTURE1 URL'>
    <img src='PASTE PICTURE1 URL'>
</a>

<a href='PASTE PICTURE2 URL'>
    <img src='PASTE PICTURE2 URL'>
</a>

<a href='PASTE PICTURE3 URL'>
        <img src='PASTE PICTURE3 URL'>
</a>

<a href='PASTE PICTURE4 URL'>
        <img src='PASTE PICTURE4 URL'>
</a>

</html>
```

Start the style section.

Set the page background (see page 20).

Choose the margin between each picture. Set the height to 160px so all images line up nicely. The white 20px border will look like a picture frame.

Type <a href=' . Next paste in the image URL you copied in step 1. Then type '>.

Type <img src=' . Then paste in the image URL and type '>.

Type </a> to close the link.

⚠ RESPECTING COPYRIGHT

Copyright means the legal ownership of something. You need to think about who owns the images you are linking to or downloading. There shouldn't be any major issues unless you try to make a website available to the public. Do check with an adult to make sure.

An alternative is to find a free to use image: search for an image, then look for the **Settings** button on the website results page. Click **Advanced Search** then look for **Usage Rights**. On this menu choose **Free to use, share or modify**.

Save and test your code after adding each image. Look up and down the text editor for patterns in your code to keep it bug-free.

GEOGRAPHY QUIZ

There are lots of ways you can build a quiz using HTML. We are going to make our quiz really interesting by using some animation to reveal the answer. There is a special feature of CSS that allows us to change a property, such as colour, to create animation. We can also use this feature to make the answer spin and reveal itself slowly.

STEP 1 – PLANNING

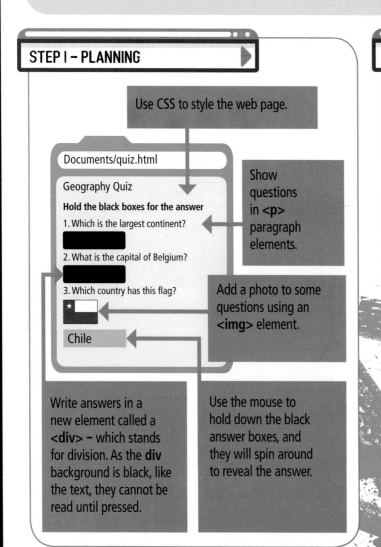

Use CSS to style the web page.

Documents/quiz.html

Geography Quiz

Hold the black boxes for the answer

1. Which is the largest continent?

2. What is the capital of Belgium?

3. Which country has this flag?

Chile

Show questions in **<p>** paragraph elements.

Add a photo to some questions using an **<img>** element.

Write answers in a new element called a **<div>** – which stands for division. As the **div** background is black, like the text, they cannot be read until pressed.

Use the mouse to hold down the black answer boxes, and they will spin around to reveal the answer.

STEP 2 – DOWNLOAD PICTURES

⇨ Decide on a topic for the quiz. In this example we will use geography, but you could choose something else.

Chilean flag | Search

⇨ Search for any photos you need.

⇨ Right-click one image.

⇨ Click **Save Image As**.

⇨ Navigate to your **Documents** folder then click **Save**.

CUSTOMISE

- Add more questions. A good quiz needs at least ten.
- Include more images for some questions.
- Make a multiple choice question with several possible answers.
- Experiment with different colour values for the div:active section.
- Alter the value 1800 to 180 or 3600. What changes when you press an answer div?

⇨ Start your text editor, or click **File** > **New File**.

⇨ Here is the code for the whole page. Type in the HTML tags and the style section, followed by the first question. Save your code as **quiz.html**, then open in your browser and test it. If it works, add the remaining questions one at a time.

Sublime Text

```
<html>

<style>
    body{margin:20px;
        background-color:lightblue;}
    p{font-size:16px;}
    div{
        background-color:black;
        width:120px; height:40px;
        text-align:center;
        line-height:40px;
        font-size:16px;
        transition:all 2s;}

    div:active{
        background-color:lightgreen;
        transform:rotate(1800deg);}
</style>

<h1>Geography Quiz</h1>
<h3>Hold the black boxes for the answer</h3>

<p>1. Which is the largest continent?</p>
<div>Asia</div>

<p>2. What is the capital of Belgium?</p>
<div>Brussels</div>

<p>3. Which country has this flag?</p>
<img src='chile_flag.png'>
<br>
<div>Chile</div>

</html>
```

Start the style section.

Put some space around all elements with a 20 pixel margin.

Add background colour for the page.
Add the font size for the questions.
 Add the div element to hold the answers.

Add the div's starting colour.
 Add the div's starting size.
Centre the answer text in the div.

Animate the div smoothly over two seconds if the div changes any of its properties.

Define the div when it is active and the mouse is pressed on it.

Turn the div green.

Rotate the div 1800 degrees (five complete rotations).

Use a <p> for each question and a <div> for the answer.

Add <img> after the <p> for any pictures you want to include.

 **KEY CONCEPT**

ACTIVE
• When the mouse is pressed down over an element, you define properties for that element by using the **:active** code. In this activity, **div** is the element that reveals the answer when the mouse is pressed over it.

TRANSITION
• The code transition makes specific properties change slowly. In this activity, the **div** reveals its answer slowly, like an animation.

 Now view your web page!

⟩ PIZZA DELIVERY

We have seen how input elements can be used to let users enter information on a web page (page 16). In this project, we will apply those techniques to create a web page to order your own perfect pizza. (You will have to cook it yourself though!)

(page 16)

STEP 1 – PLANNING

Style the page with CSS.

Use a photo of a pizza in an **<img>** element.

Use radio buttons to let people select which type of pizza base they want.

Use a drop-down menu to select the type of cheese.

Choose additional toppings with checkboxes.

Documents/pizza.html

Max's Pizza Shop

Delivery

Choose your base:
- ● Classic
- ○ Cheese
- ○ Crisp

Cheese type:

Mozzarella ⬍

Toppings:

☑ Ham   ☐ Peppers   ☑ Mushrooms

STEP 2 – FIND A PICTURE

⇨ Download a photo of a pizza into your **Documents** folder.

⇨ Search for a pizza photo.   ⇨ Right-click one photo.   ⇨ Click **Save Image As**.   ⇨ Navigate to your **Documents** folder then click **Save**.

⇨ Start your text editor, or click **File** > **New File**.

⇨ Start coding your pizza shop. Begin with the HTML tags and then work through the code. Stop after each section, **Save** and test your code. Call the file **pizza.html**.

Sublime Text

```html
<html>
<style>
    body{font-size:14px;
        font-family:Arial;
        background-color:red;
        margin:40px;}
</style>

<h1 style='color:white'>Max's Pizza Shop</h1>
<img width="300" src="pizza.jpg">
<h3>Delivery</h3>

<p>Choose your base:</p>
<input name="base" type="radio">Classic<br>
<input name="base" type="radio">Cheese<br>
<input name="base" type="radio">Crisp<br>

<br>

<p>Cheese type:</p>
<select style="font-size: 24px;">
        <option>Mozzarella</option>
        <option>Cheddar</option>
        <option>No cheese</option>
</select>

<p>Toppings:</p>
<input type="checkbox"> Ham
<input type="checkbox"> Peppers
<input type="checkbox"> Mushrooms
</html>
```

Start the style section.

Add styling in the body section. Most of the input elements will pick up this styling too. To make it clearer to read your code, press enter after each semi-colon.

Use inline styling to set the colour for the heading.

Use the picture downloaded from step 1. Adjust the width if necessary.

Set the name of each radio button input to be the same. This makes sure only one can be selected.

Start a new line.

Add a select element for the drop-down menu to choose the cheese. Each type of cheese needs a new option element.

Add a checkbox input element for each additional topping. This will let the person using the web page tick one or more options. The radio button only lets you select one.

Now view your web page!

CUSTOMISE

- Spend some time trying out different colour, font and size changes in the style section.
- Add extra toppings and some more photos to show the different toppings available.
- Add a text input box to allow people to type in any extra requests.
- Create another heading and section on the page for drinks.
- Look for a suitable image to use as a background for the page.

› SPORTS MINI-SITE

In this project you are going to learn how to make a mini website. Rather than just one page, you will build several pages with information about different sports, and one index page that will contain links to each of the individual sports pages.

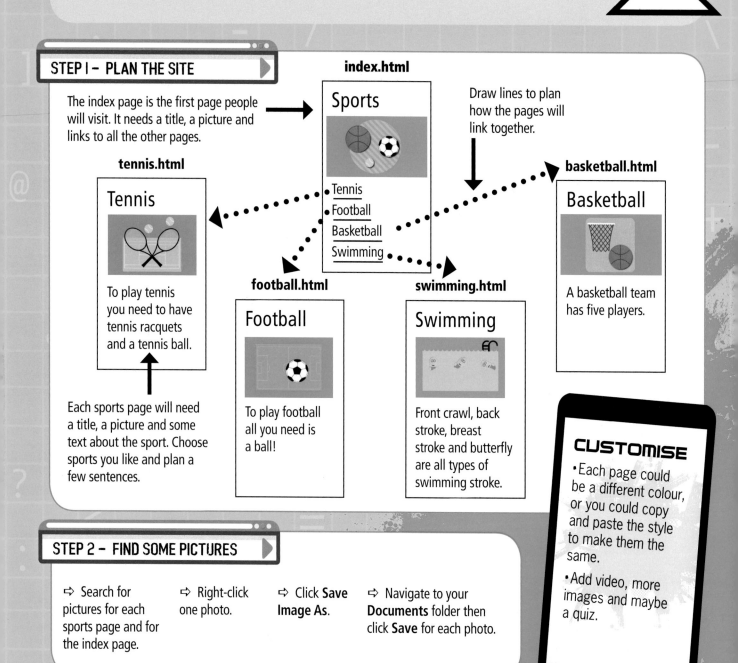

STEP 1 – PLAN THE SITE

The index page is the first page people will visit. It needs a title, a picture and links to all the other pages.

Draw lines to plan how the pages will link together.

index.html

Sports

Tennis
Football
Basketball
Swimming

tennis.html

Tennis

To play tennis you need to have tennis racquets and a tennis ball.

Each sports page will need a title, a picture and some text about the sport. Choose sports you like and plan a few sentences.

football.html

Football

To play football all you need is a ball!

swimming.html

Swimming

Front crawl, back stroke, breast stroke and butterfly are all types of swimming stroke.

basketball.html

Basketball

A basketball team has five players.

CUSTOMISE

• Each page could be a different colour, or you could copy and paste the style to make them the same.

• Add video, more images and maybe a quiz.

STEP 2 – FIND SOME PICTURES

⇨ Search for pictures for each sports page and for the index page.

⇨ Right-click one photo.

⇨ Click **Save Image As**.

⇨ Navigate to your **Documents** folder then click **Save** for each photo.

STEP 3 – START THE INDEX PAGE

⇨ Carefully type this code to start your index page:

Sublime Text

```
<html>
<h1>Sports</h1>
<img src='sport.png' width='200'><br>
<a href='tennis.html'>Tennis</a> <br>
<a href='football.html'>Football</a> <br>
<a href='basketball.html'>Basketball</a> <br>
<a href='swimming.html'>Swimming</a>
</html>
```

Add a main heading.

Use the image from step 2.

Each page will need its own link. Use <a> tags, typing the filename as the value for the href attribute. Type the name of the sport before the closing tag </a>. Use <br> tags to make each link start on a new line.

⇨ Save the page as **index.html**. Find it in your **Documents** folder and double-click it to see how it looks. Try clicking one of the links. You will get an error saying **Your file was not found**, so we need to start building these other pages.

⇨ Click the back button to return to your index.

KEY CONCEPT

STEP 4 – START THE TENNIS PAGE

⇨ Carefully type this code to start the tennis page:

Sublime Text

```
<html>
<h1>Tennis</h1>
<img src='tennis-game.jpeg'>
<p>To play tennis you need to have tennis racquets and a tennis ball.</p>
</html>
```

WEBSITES AND RELATIVE LINKS

Websites are multiple pages linked together with "a" tags. We use relative links to do this, just by typing the file name without 'http' or any web address. This is because all pages and files will be in the same folder.

Use the name of the tennis photo from step 2.

Use a <p> tag and then start typing what you know about tennis. You can always add more text later. Don't worry if it spills over the edge of the page.

Save the page as **tennis.html**. In your browser, try clicking the link to **Tennis**. It should now take you to your new page!

STEP 5 – MORE PAGES

⇨ Repeat step 4 for each of the other sports. Take care to type the name of the picture file carefully. After you complete each page, save it with name of the sport followed by **.html**, then test your index page again.

GLOSSARY

ANIMATION Making elements on a web page move or fade in or out.

ATTRIBUTE Extra information about an HTML element, such as the address of an image.

BROWSER A program used to view web pages, such as Chrome or Internet Explorer.

BUG An error in a web page that stops it displaying correctly.

COPYRIGHT Rules and laws protecting the person who created an image or piece of work.

CSS (CASCADING STYLE SHEETS) The language used to describe how HTML elements will look.

DEBUG Removing bugs (or errors) from an HTML page.

DOCUMENTS FOLDER One of the main folders used to store files on a computer.

ELEMENT One of the objects making up a web page, such as a paragraph or image.

EMBEDDING Placing an element on one web page, but getting its content from a different website.

HEXADECIMAL A system of numbers based on 16s, using digits from 0 to 9, then A to F.

HOST To be accessed by, or made available to, the public.

HTML (HYPERTEXT MARKUP LANGUAGE) The language used to build web pages.

INPUT A way to get information into a web page or computer.

LINK/HYPERLINK A clickable link from one web page to another.

MARGIN The space around an HTML element.

PROPERTY Information about the style of an element, such as its colour or size.

REFRESH To load a web page again in the browser, so changes to the page can be seen.

RGB The system used to mix Red, Green and Blue light to make any colour.

STYLE Information written in CSS describing things like the size and colour of an element.

TAGS Special words in an HTML document surrounded by angle brackets <> defining an element.

TEXT EDITOR A program used to create and change text, such as the code used to build a web page.

THUMBNAIL A small image that links to a larger image when clicked.

URL (UNIFORM RESOURCE LOCATOR) The address of a file on the web.

WEB STANDARDS

Modern web browsers will still show parts of your HTML even if there are bugs in it. However, you should try and code everything correctly as errors can creep in.

Once you start to publish your web pages, you will need to check your code works on other browsers (see page 4) and on different sized screens.

> BUGS AND DEBUGGING

When you find your code is not working as expected, stop and look through each command you have put in. Think about what you want it to do, and what it is really telling the computer to do. If you are entering one of the programs in this book, check you have not missed a line. Here are some things to watch out for:

Use tags correctly:

```
<h1>A
<h1>B
<h1>C
```
✗

```
<h1>A</h1>
<h1>B</h1>
<h1>C</h1>
```
✓

Most elements need an opening and closing tag.

Use tags correctly:

```
<p>Line 1
Line 2
Line 3</p>
```
✗

```
<p>Line 1</p>
<p>Line 2</p>
<p>Line 3</p>
```
✓

Typing enter in your code won't start a new line on your web page.

Close tags:

```
<p>Hello<p>
```
✗

```
<p>Hello</p>
```
✓

Closing tags need a forward slash symbol.

Take care with quotes:

```
<p style="color:red;>Pizza</p>
```
✗

```
<p style="color:red';>Pizza</p>
```
✗

```
<p style="color:red;>"Pizza</p>
```
✗

```
<p style="color:red;">Pizza</p>
```
✓

Quotes always work in pairs. Make sure they match and are in the correct place.

Check URLs:

```
<a href='pgae2.htlm'>
```
✗

```
<a href='page2.html'>
```
✓

Type all URLs carefully and check they are correct.

Type commands carefully:

```
<imge sorc='pic.png'>
```
✗

```
<img src='pic.png'>
```
✓

Make sure you spell tags correctly.

TIPS TO REDUCE BUGS

If you are making your own web page, spend time drawing a diagram and planning it before you start. Try changing values if things don't work, and don't be afraid to start again – you will learn from it.

Practise debugging! Make a very simple web page and get a friend to change one line of code while you're not looking. Can you fix it?

When things are working properly, spend time looking through your code so you understand each line. Experiment and change your code, and try out different values. To be good at debugging, you need to understand what each line of your code does and how it works.

INDEX

First published in Great Britain in 2017 by Wayland

Text copyright © ICT Apps Ltd, 2017
Art and design copyright © Hodder and Stoughton Limited, 2017

All rights reserved.

Editor: Catherine Brereton
Freelance editor: Hayley Fairhead
Designer: Peter Clayman
Illustrator: Maria Cox

ISBN: 978 1 5263 0105 5
10 9 8 7 6 5 4 3 2 1

MIX
Paper from responsible sources
FSC® C104740
FSC www.fsc.org

Wayland
An imprint of
Hachette Children's Group
Part of Hodder & Stoughton
Carmelite House
50 Victoria Embankment
London EC4Y 0DZ

An Hachette UK Company
www.hachette.co.uk
www.hachettechildrens.co.uk

Printed in China

The website addresses (URLs) included in this book were valid at the time of going to press. However, it is possible that contents or addresses may have changed since the publication of this book. No responsibility for any such changes can be accepted by either the author or the Publisher.

E-safety
Children will need access to the internet for most of the activities in this book. Parents or teachers should supervise this and discuss staying safe online with children.